P9-BIQ-087

ides: 2

MAMMALS

OF THE

SAN FRANCISCO BAY REGION

BY

WILLIAM D. AND ELIZABETH BERRY

ILLUSTRATED BY WILLIAM D. BERRY

UNIVERSITY OF CALIFORNIA PRESS

BERKELEY AND LOS ANGELES: 1959

CALIFORNIA NATURAL HISTORY GUIDES

General Editor: Arthur C. Smith

Introduction to the Natural History of the San Francisco
Bay Region

Mammals of the San Francisco Bay Region

Reptiles and Amphibians of the San Francisco Bay Region

Native Trees of the San Francisco Bay Region

UNIVERSITY OF CALIFORNIA PRESS

BERKELEY AND LOS ANGELES, CALIFORNIA

© 1959 BY

THE REGENTS OF THE UNIVERSITY OF CALIFORNIA

PRINTED IN THE UNITED STATES OF AMERICA

LIBRARY OF CONGRESS CATALOG CARD NUMBER: 59-6052

DESIGNED BY JOHN B. GOETZ

CONTENTS

INTRODUCTION

Of the more than two hundred different species of mammals found in California, seventy-five live in the bay region. They range from shrews that weigh less than an eighth of an ounce to mountain lions that may weigh two hundred pounds, and include such animals as jack rabbits, porpoises, bats, and man. These and all other mammals have two characteristics in common: they nurse their young, and at some time in their lives they have hair or fur.

The large number of different mammals found in the bay region is partly explained by the varied character of the land and vegetation. There are redwood forests, with an abundance of water and vegetation (pl. 1). Oak woodland and dense thickets of shrubs

or small trees, known as chaparral, are typical of the bay region foothills (pls. 3, 6). Dry, grass-covered hills spotted with oaks (pl. 8), fresh- and salt-water marshes (pl. 2), and even cities themselves provide suitable habitats for many mammals.

Unlike the early settlers of California, we are no longer dependent on wildlife as a source of food and fur, and individually, these mammals may seem to be of little value to man. Today, however, we know that animals are valuable in other ways—we know that the relationship of each species to its enviroment is important to us. For example, the coyote is a well-known predator that has long been hunted and poisoned in our agricultural areas. But in these same areas, we have had to take protective measures against crop damage by jack rabbits and pocket gophers. Since the coyote eats rabbits and rodents, should he be considered harmful or beneficial? There are many questions like this that can be answered only by further study of wildlife.

The California grizzly bear, the emblem of our state, used to be fairly common in the bay region. Vaqueros, the Spanish cowboys, even lassoed them for sport. Today this species is extinct. As the land was settled, the dangerous and sometimes destructive grizzlies were shot and poisoned until the last one disappeared. It is unfortunate that a few do not remain to be seen in our national parks, but our present attitude toward conservation came too late. Fortunately, California citizens realized the value of their wildlife before many animals met the same fate. Today, in Muir Woods, East Bay Regional Parks, Alum Rock Park, and many other places where wildlife is protected, all of us have an opportunity to see the mammals described in this book.

[6]

On pages 70-72 is a check list that includes all species of mammals that have been found in the counties surrounding San Francisco, San Pablo, and Suisun bays. The text describes the forty-eight most common land mammals found in this area. Species accounts are brief, with identification, habitat, range, breeding habits, and food summarized for each animal described. The paintings and many sketches, taken from life, show these mammals as they are ordinarily seen. Following the species accounts is a section on activities that will help you to appreciate mammals in the bay region.

Mule Deer or Black-tailed Deer (*Odocoileus hemionus columbianus*)

Deer are wary, but there are many places in the bay region, near cities and in parks where they are given protection, where they may be seen. Your chances of seeing wild deer may be better in Muir Woods or the Berkeley Hills than in more remote parts of California.

Bucks and does may be found together throughout the fall and winter, but in the spring the does wander off to bear their young. The doe hides her fawns in a thicket or under similar cover. In the sunlight that filters through the leaves a fawn's spotted coat blends with the background of light and dark. Camouflaged this way, a fawn is very difficult to see.

By fall the fawns usually lose their spots and grow brownish winter coats like their mothers. In the summer these yearlings shed their long winter hair and acquire the shorter, reddish summer coats of adult Black-tails.

A young buck begins to grow antlers the first winter, but his first pair is usually single spikes. The

antlers are shed each year in late winter, and new antlers start to grow in the spring. By early summer the new antlers are well grown, but covered with short hair, or "velvet." As they mature and harden, the velvet dies and is scraped off against shrubs or saplings. Each successive pair of antlers is larger, until the animal is approximately five or six years old. Very old bucks, however, may have fewer points than they had in their prime.

By fall the bucks are in their prime and are ready to battle over mates. Rivals lunge and spar, but usually the fights are brief, with one of the bucks retreating to seek another doe.

Identification: Approximately 3 ft. high at shoulder; tail entirely black on upper surface. *Habitat:* Forests, open woodland, and chaparral. Beds down in thickets during the day. *Range:* Throughout the bay region. *Young:* 1 to 3 (usually 2) born in spring or early summer. *Food:* Grass, foliage, twigs, fruits, and acorns.

RABBITS AND HARES

Rabbits and hares, although gnawing mammals, are not rodents but belong to a separate order, Lagomorpha. In the bay region there are two rabbits and one hare.

Desert Cottontail (*Sylvilagus auduboni*)

In a cottontail's zigzag dash to safety his white tail flashes conspicuously, then suddenly vanishes. The rabbit seems to disappear, for the instant he turns or stops the white is hidden, and his grizzled coloration blends with the surroundings. He "freezes," motionless except for an occasional twitch of his nose. If he is pursued, he seeks safety in a blackberry thicket or similar protection. Although cottontails feed in the open, they are never far from cover. The rabbits sometimes damage crops, but if fence lines are free of brush the area is usually too unprotected for their liking.

Identification: Smaller than the jack rabbit. Grizzled gray with conspicuous white tail; underparts white. Head and body 12 to 15 in. long; ear 3 to 4 in. long. *Habitat:* Riverbottom thickets or open plains

with scattered brush. Makes home in burrow or well-sheltered, shallow depression, called a "form"; nest lined with fur. *Range:* Throughout the bay region, except north coastal areas. *Young:* 2 or more litters a year; 2 to 6 in a litter. *Food:* Grasses, shrubs, cultivated plants and fruits.

Brush Rabbit (*Sylvilagus bachmani*)

This small, drab edition of the cottontail never strays more than a few yards from cover, but usually follows one of his many tunnel-like trails through the vegetation. Brush Rabbits are readily observed in such protected areas as Golden Gate Park.

Identification: Darker and smaller than cottontail, with relatively smaller ears. Tail not conspicuously white; underparts grayish. Head and body 11 to 13 in. long; ear 2 to 2⅖ in. long. *Habitat:* Prefers chaparral and forest margins. Well-hidden nest lined with dry grass and fur. *Range:* Throughout the bay region. *Young:* Apparently one litter a year; 2 to 5 in a litter. *Food:* Grasses and roots.

Black-tailed Jack Rabbit (*Lepus californicus*)

Anyone who has ever driven through the valleys and foothills has seen the long-eared jack rabbit bounding across grassy open areas. The jack rabbit, which is technically not a rabbit but a hare, is one of the fastest animals in North America, and his great speed is his best protection. The jack rabbit's home is nothing more than a scratched-out hollow or depression in the ground where he can crouch and be shielded by tall grass or brush. He crouches with his legs folded under him and his ears laid flat along his back; this position makes it difficult for his enemies to see him. If one gets too close, the jack leaps from his hiding place. The sudden leap startles the enemy, and this gives the jack rabbit a good running start. Only a fast dog or coyote can overtake him, and even then he frequently escapes by jumping straight up in the air or quickly changing directions (see pl. 8).

Baby jack rabbits are able to hop when they are only a few hours old. Unlike the blind and helpless baby cottontails, the little jacks are born well furred and their eyes open soon after they are born.

Jack rabbits are serious pests because they feed on the same ranges as sheep and cattle. Although the amount of food eaten by one jack rabbit is small, the total quantity consumed by thousands of them is tremendous. They multiply rapidly, especially if their natural enemies—coyotes, bobcats, large birds of prey—are destroyed. When these enemies of the rabbits are left to roam unchecked, they keep the rabbit population down.

Identification: Large black-tipped ears; tail black on top. Head and body 17 to 21 in. long; ear 6 to 7 in. long. Weighs 3 to 7 lbs. *Habitat:* Prefers open slopes or broken chaparral-grassland. *Range:* Dry inland areas. *Young:* 1 to 3 litters a year; 3 to 8 in a litter. *Food:* Grasses, herbs, shrubs, and cultivated plants.

The rodents, or gnawing mammals, found in the bay region are rats, mice, gophers, squirrels, chipmunks, and Aplodontia.

Norway Rat (*Rattus norvegicus*)

Rats eat and contaminate millions of dollars' worth of stored food and grain each year. In addition, rats and their insect parasites may carry serious diseases. One of these, plague, is carried by fleas found on both introduced and native rodents.

A rodent introduced from the Old World, the Norway Rat is adaptable, aggressive, and very difficult to combat on a small scale. Only by destroying their breeding places, removing food supplies, and thoroughly ratproofing all buildings can these rats be controlled.

Although of no benefit in the wild form, a special variety of albino (white) Norway Rats are useful to man as laboratory animals.

Identification: Grayish-brown color; naked, scaly

Norway Rat   *Black Rat*

tail, shorter than head and body. Head and body 7 to 10 in. long; tail 5 to 8 in. long. *Habitat:* Cities, farmland, and marshes. Usually remains near ground level. Nest of fiber, paper, etc., in buildings or burrows. *Range:* Throughout bay region. *Young:* Several litters a year; 4 to 12 (average 7) in a litter. *Food:* Anything edible: grain, meat, stored foods, etc.

Black Rat, Roof Rat (*Rattus rattus*)

Like the Norway Rat, this Old World species is well established in California. The Black Rat is a good climber and sometimes reaches otherwise inaccessible areas on buildings by traveling across power lines.

Identification: Brown with light underparts, or entirely black. Tail longer than head and body. Head and body 6 to 7 in. long; tail 8½ to 10 in. long. *Habitat:* Coastal cities, farmland, and wooded streams. Climbs readily; often nests in trees. Nest of fibers, paper, etc. *Range:* Throughout bay region. *Young:* Several litters a year; average 6 in a litter. *Food:* Same as that of Norway Rat.

House Mouse (*Mus musculus*)

These mice and their relatives, the Norway and Black
Rats, are Old World rodents that arrived in America
as stowaways on the first ships from Europe. Only
distantly related to our native rats and mice, these
invaders are unique in their dependence on man and
his activities. House Mice are adaptable and often
live in fields and waste places, but they are primarily
household pests. In their search for food and nest
material, they spoil our food, gnaw holes in fabrics,
and leave an offensive odor. Mice can be poisoned
and trapped, but the most effective way of discourag-
ing them is to store all food in tightly covered metal or
glass containers.

Identification: Small; grayish-brown body, grayish or
buffy underparts; scaly tail. Head and body 3⅕ to 3⅖
in. long; tail 2⅘ to 3⅘ in. long. *Habitat:* Usually
around buildings, but sometimes in fields, brushy
places, and salt marshes. Home is a nest of shredded
paper, cloth, or fibers, hidden in a dark place. *Range:*
Throughout bay region. *Young:* Several litters a year;
5 to 7 in a litter. *Food:* Anything edible: grain, meat,
and stored foods.

Western Harvest Mouse
(*Reithrodontomys megalotis*)

Dense grass and weeds hide the tiny harvest mice. Their nests, neatly woven little balls of dry grass, are often discovered under old boards or matted vegetation. Harvest mice are active at night, appearing equally at home in runways or in the tangle of stems and twigs overhead (see pl. 5).

Identification: Yellowish-brown coat. Head and body $2\frac{4}{5}$ to 3 in. long; tail $2\frac{1}{2}$ to $3\frac{1}{5}$ in. long. Incisor teeth grooved (see sketch B). Teeth of House Mice not grooved (sketch A). *Habitat:* Prefers moist, grassy areas or shaded slopes; open to semiopen ground. Nest is a ball of grass above ground or in burrow. *Range:* Throughout the bay region. *Young:* May have several litters a year; 3 to 7 (average 4) in a litter. *Food:* Seeds, fruit, grain, and green vegetation.

Salt-marsh Harvest Mouse
(*Reithrodontomys raviventris*)

Identification: Similar to Western Harvest Mouse. Rich brown; rusty belly. Head and body $2\frac{3}{5}$ to $3\frac{1}{5}$ in. long; tail $2\frac{1}{5}$ to $3\frac{2}{5}$ in. long. *Habitat and range:* Salt marshes of bay region only.

Western Harvest Mouse

Deer Mouse (*Peromyscus maniculatus*)

The name "Deer Mouse" is fitting for these big-eared rodents (pl. 5). The reddish-brown coat, white underparts, and short hair covering the tail distinguish them from the city-dwelling House Mice. Deer Mice belong to the group called white-footed mice, found in all parts of the United States. They are usually the most numerous mammals in their chosen habitat. Deer Mice are found in redwood groves, chaparral, and grassland; in fact, everywhere there is suitable cover except in the marshes.

Despite their abundance, they are not often seen, because of their nocturnal habits. These mice are an important part of the diet of predators, large and small, including fur-bearers such as the fox and bobcat. People with summer cabins are often aware of Deer Mice, for they may help themselves to food and shred clothing to line their nests.

Identification: Brown above, white underparts; tail bicolored. Head and body 2⅖ to 4 in. long; tail 2 to 5 in. long; ear less than ½ in. long. *Habitat:* Wherever suitable cover exists, except tidal marshes. Nest of dry grass or plant down, under logs or rocks, or in burrows. *Range:* Throughout the bay region. *Young:* 3 to 4 litters a year; 2 to 7 in a litter. *Food:* Seeds, acorns, grain, berries, and some insects.

Piñon Mouse (*Peromyscus truei*)

Identification: Grayish brown above; ears very large. Head and body $3\frac{3}{5}$ to 4 in. long; tail $3\frac{2}{5}$ to $4\frac{4}{5}$ in. long. *Habitat:* Prefers chaparral and rocky areas. Avoids open grassland, dense forests, and salt marshes. *Range:* Throughout the bay region.

California Mouse (*Peromyscus californicus*)

Identification: Dark brown above; blackish tail. Largest of the *Peromyscus* group. Head and body $3\frac{4}{5}$ to $4\frac{3}{5}$ in. long; tail 5 to $5\frac{4}{5}$ in. long. *Habitat:* Prefers heavy chaparral-oak association. Frequently builds nests in wood-rat houses. *Range:* Bay region south of Carquinez Strait.

California Mouse

Dusky-footed Wood Rat, Pack Rat
(*Neotoma fuscipes*)

Wood rats spend countless hours working on their houses—the familiar stick-pile lodges often seen under the chaparral or among the branches of trees. One house may have successive owners, each adding new sticks until the pile may be more than six feet high. These old houses are quite complex inside, containing many hallways and several abandoned nests in addition to those occupied at the moment. The nest, usually a cup-shaped mass of shredded bark, is the wood rat's sleeping quarters. Many wood-rat houses have mice living in the abandoned hallways (pl. 6). Chinks and crevices between sticks sometimes afford shelter for lizards, salamanders, slugs, snails, and insects.

Wood rats are frequently called "trade" or "pack" rats. They may collect all sorts of apparently useless objects, such as jar lids, cigarette wrappers and old newspaper, which they carry away to their houses. This "collecting" habit has made them a nuisance around camps and cabins, but generally they go unnoticed. These rodents are most active at night, and are rarely seen by day unless their houses are disturbed. Wood rats are more attractive looking (pl. 4) and lack the aggressive dispositions of Old World rats.

Wood-rat house

Identification: Gray-brown above, white below; tail is haired. Hind feet dusky above. Head and body 7⅗ to 9 in. long; tail 6⅘ to 8⅔ in. long. *Habitat:* Prefers heavy chaparral or woods. House is a bulky pile of sticks in trees or on the ground; nest of shredded bark inside the house. *Range:* Throughout the bay region. *Young:* May have more than one litter a year; 3 to 4 in a litter. *Food:* Acorns, seeds. leaves, grain, roots, and fruits.

Desert Wood Rat (*Neotoma lepida*)

Identification: Smaller and paler than Dusky-footed Wood Rat; tan above, white or buffy below. Head and body 5⅘ to 7 in. long; tail 4⅓ to 6⅖ in. long. *Habitat:* Sparse chaparral or rocky areas, cliff crevices. House is usually less conspicuous than that of the Dusky-footed Wood Rat. Frequently places nest in caves or tunnels, often with no attempt at house building. *Range:* Mount Diablo south; chaparral of inner Coast Ranges.

California Vole, California Meadow Mouse
(*Microtus californicus*)

Many of the grass-covered hills, and often pastures and marshes as well, are scenes of constant rodent activity. The grass is honeycombed with neat tunnels, built and maintained by meadow mice (pl. 5). The floors of these tunnels are smooth and well packed from daily use, and any debris in them is cleared away, for a meadow mouse's life often depends on a speedy and unobstructed retreat.

These field mice, as they are frequently called, invade farmlands, but they avoid buildings. Their burrows and surface tunnels provide all the shelter needed. At times these mice become excessively abundant and cause great damage to crops. Hay and grain fields may be riddled with burrows and runways, and in eating green food and cutting roots and stems to make tunnels, meadow mice may destroy a large part of a crop. The mice also damage orchards by gnawing the bark and roots of trees.

Meadow mice have large families, and they have them often. Each young mouse can take care of itself at the age of two weeks, so it is easy to understand why the species sometimes reaches great numbers. Fortunately, many predators—hawks, owls, snakes,

weasels, skunks, badgers, foxes, coyotes, and bobcats —aid in keeping the mouse population in check. Without a high reproduction rate, the species would not survive. Encouraging and protecting the natural enemies of meadow mice help to keep the population down and thus reduce the damage they cause.

Identification: Short tail; grizzled, gray-brown coat; ears nearly hidden by fur. Head and body $4\frac{3}{4}$ to $5\frac{2}{3}$ in. long; tail $1\frac{3}{4}$ to $2\frac{4}{5}$ in. long. *Habitat:* Prefers moist stream sides, grassy meadowlike areas, and salt marshes. Avoids heavily grazed grassland. *Range:* Throughout the bay region. *Young:* Several litters a year; 2 to 9 (average 5) in a litter. *Food:* Grasses, seeds, tender shoots, roots, and bark.

Heermann Kangaroo Rat (*Dipodomys heermanni*)

Kangaroo rats are primarily desert animals, but in the bay region are found in grassland or under sparse chaparral. They rely on their speed and leaping ability to escape enemies. Kangaroo rats move on their hind legs, with their long tails trailing behind for balance and their tiny forepaws tucked out of sight under their chins. Front feet are used mainly for digging and gathering food. Finding water is no problem for these rodents, as the chemical decomposition of food provides all the liquid they need. Kangaroo rats often settle disputes with one another by pairing off (pl. 7) and fighting with powerful kicks of their hind feet.

Identification: Long hind legs; long, tufted tail; external cheek pouches. Head and body 4 to 5 in. long; tail 6½ to 8½ in. long. *Habitat:* Open country; grassland and chaparral. Nest of dry grass in extensive burrow system. *Range:* North from Nicasio, Marin County, and Vacaville. South from Berkeley and Mount Diablo. *Young:* One litter a year; 2 to 4 in a litter. *Food:* Seeds, grain, and some green plants.

California Pocket Mouse
(*Perognathus californicus*)

The pocket mouse is well named. His fur-lined "pockets," one on each side of his mouth, may bulge with seeds until the mouse looks as if he had the mumps. At night pocket mice forage under the chaparral on dry foothill slopes, gathering small seeds and grain (pl. 5). When their pockets are filled, the mice return to their burrows, where they store the seeds in small pits along the passageways. A mouse empties his pockets, or pouches, by pushing forward with his forepaws, sometimes turning his pockets wrong side out to remove the remaining seeds.

Identification: Olive-brown coloration; spinelike hairs on rump. Head and body $3\frac{1}{5}$ to $3\frac{1}{2}$ in. long; tail 4 to $5\frac{1}{5}$ in. long. *Habitat:* Open and semiopen country; slopes with light chaparral. Nest in underground burrow system. *Range:* North of San Francisco Bay; not found near coast. *Young:* Possibly more than one litter a year; 4 to 7 in a litter. *Food:* Seeds.

San Joaquin Pocket Mouse
(*Perognathus inornatus*)

Identification: Pale buffy coloration, silky fur (no spines). Head and body $2\frac{1}{2}$ to $3\frac{1}{5}$ in. long; tail $2\frac{4}{5}$ to 3 in. long. *Habitat:* Dry, open, grassy or weedy ground, or sandy soil. *Range:* Foothills bordering San Joaquin Valley.

California Pocket Mouse

Botta Pocket Gopher (*Thomomys bottae*)

Overnight a pocket gopher can ruin the appearance of a lawn or garden. In digging his tunnels, he pushes the familiar mounds of dirt to the surface. A lawn dotted with these mounds may look as if it has been invaded by several of these animals, but a single gopher can cover a wide area. A gardener may try to eliminate this pest by flooding or fumigating, but since the burrows are extensive and may be plugged with earth, the water or gas often never reaches the gopher. The use of a trap or poisoned bait is most effective, if it is placed in one of the gopher's main tunnels. The lateral feeding tunnels (see sketch below) are usually plugged, so care should be taken to dig to the main passageway, which is left open.

Except in the mating season, gophers are rarely found in the open, preferring to remain in safety underground. Strong claws and chisel teeth equip them for a life of burrowing. In hard soils they literally gnaw their way through the ground. A gopher's in-

cisors remain outside his mouth even when his lips are closed; this keeps dirt out of his mouth while he is digging. After he has loosened enough soil, the gopher turns and pushes it back along the tunnel with his chin and chest, like a miniature bulldozer.

Gophers are vegetarians, and find an abuandance of food in our fields and gardens. The rodents store more than they eat, cutting the food into small pieces and carrying it in their fur-lined cheek pouches to underground storerooms. Although individual damage may be small, the total gopher population destroys millions of dollars' worth of crops each year. Gophers are caught at their burrow entrances by coyotes, foxes, bobcats, and owls; a weasel (see pl. 2) or gopher snake can pursue one into its tunnel.

Identification: Brown; feet and tail whitish. Short, thick tail; small ears and eyes; cheek pouches. Head and body 4⅘ to 7 in. long; tail 2 to 3¾ in. long. *Habitat:* Semiopen to open areas; avoids hard soils and wet areas. Nest of fibers and grasses in deep tunnel. *Range:* Throughout the bay region. *Young:* Usually one litter a year; 1 to 13 (average 5) in a litter. *Food:* Roots, bulbs, tubers, green stalks, and grain.

Western Gray Squirrel (*Sciurus griseus*)

A born acrobat, the gray squirrel bounds along small branches or leaps through space, maintaining balance with his plumelike tail. Because of their conspicuous appearance and the fact that they are active by day throughout the year, these squirrels are well known (pl. 4). They make their homes in redwood forests and oak woodlands, where their bulky nests, somewhat resembling arboreal nests of wood rats (see p. 21), are often seen in the treetops.

Acorns, the squirrel's chief food, are collected and stored in shallow holes or caches, in the forest floor. These caches are apparently found by scent, but many acorns are never recovered. These acorns may sprout into new trees, and in this way the squirrel aids in replanting the trees upon which he depends. Gray squirrels occasionally raid orchards, but in general this species does little damage.

Identification: Gray body, white underparts; bushy tail. Head and body 12 in. long; tail 10 to 12 in. long. *Habitat:* Prefers open forest containing oaks. Nest made of sticks and bark (see sketch on opposite page), or it makes its home in a hollow tree. *Range:* North and east from Mount Tamalpais and Vacaville;

south from north-central San Mateo County. Absent from Mount Diablo. *Young:* One litter born in the spring; 3 to 5 in a litter. *Food:* Acorns and nuts, fungus, bird eggs.

Eastern Gray Squirrel (*Sciurus carolinensis*)

This squirrel and the following species are eastern squirrels that have been released in many city parks. Their habits are similar to those of the Western Gray Squirrel.

Identification: Smaller and browner than the Western Gray Squirrel. Head and body 8 to 10 in. long; tail 7¾ to 10 in. long. *Range:* Introduced into Golden Gate and other city parks.

Fox Squirrel (*Sciurus niger*)

Identification: Size similar to that of the Western Gray Squirrel, but has rusty color on underparts and tail. Head and body 10 to 15 in. long; tail 9 to 14 in. long. *Range:* Introduced into Golden Gate and other city parks.

Sonoma Chipmunk (*Eutamias sonomae*)

The repeated, chirping scold of a chipmunk is a common sound in the chaparral, and is easily mistaken for a bird call. The chipmunk stays near cover, and his striped pattern makes him almost indistinguishable from the branches and shadows. A sharp-eyed observer can often find the animal by watching for a movement, for at each "chirp" the chipmunk nervously jerks his tail. When the chipmunk is satisfied that the danger is past, he resumes foraging through the ground litter, stuffing seeds, nuts, and berries into his cheek pouches. Unlike the gopher and the pocket mouse, which have external pouches, the chipmunk actually carries food in his distended cheeks. When his pouches are full, he digs a small hole and empties his food supply into it, then brushes dry leaves and dirt over the cache.

Chipmunks always seem busy. They are ready to freeze or run at the slightest disturbance, for like most rodents their lives are keyed to emergency.

Identification: Dark-brown body with indistinct stripes (pl. 5). Head and body 4⅘ to 5½ in. long; tail 4 to 5 in. long. *Habitat:* Warm, dry, brushy slopes; chaparral. Nests in or under fallen logs. *Range:* Counties north of the bay. *Young:* One litter a year; 4 to 6 in a litter. *Food:* Seeds, nuts, buds, fruit, and some insects.

California Ground Squirrel (*Citellus beecheyi*)

A plump, grayish squirrel perched on a fence post or standing erect beside its burrow (pl. 4) is a familiar sight in the hills and farmlands. If approached, the squirrel dashes over the mound of earth surrounding the burrow entrance and disappears to safety below, giving a sharp trill of alarm. Despite their appealing appearance, California Ground Squirrels head the list of agricultural pests in our state. They destroy sprouting and ripening grain, dig holes in irrigation ditches, and may carry several diseases. Only a full-scale trapping and poisoning campaign over a large area can effectively destroy them. These squirrels are very alert, and often cannot be trapped or poisoned because they remain underground for long periods of time. During the dry season, from late spring through summer, many of the squirrels in the foothills bordering the Great Central Valley go into a summer sleep known as "estivation," and do not reappear until the hills turn green.

Identification: Mottled brownish-gray coat; neck and shoulders whitish. Head and body 9 to 11 in. long; tail 5 to 9 in. long. *Habitat:* Prefers open country and grassland. *Range:* Throughout the bay region. *Young:* One litter a year; 4 to 10 in a litter. *Food:* Seeds, fruit, acorns, roots, greens, and meat.

Aplodontia (*Aplodontia rufa*)

The Aplodontia, sometimes called the "Mountain Beaver," is not a beaver at all. In fact, it has no close relatives among the rodents. Its body structure resembles that of the pocket gopher, but it is much larger. It also has plushy, dark-brown fur, which is of little economic value, and a tiny stub tail.

The Aplodontia is seldom seen. The only sign of its presence may be its burrow entrances, approximately six inches in diameter. Even these holes may be obscured by dense vegetation, for the animal lives under the heavy tangle of thimbleberry, blackberry, and bracken fern often associated with redwood forests. The Aplodontia's long tunnels sometimes have streams running through them, but the nest itself is well drained and lined with dry vegetation. The piles of cut plants found near the burrow entrances may be drying for new bedding.

Identification: Large; tail almost hidden. Head and body 12 to 17 in. long; tail about 1 in. long. *Habitat:* Seepage hillsides heavily grown with fern and thimbleberry. Nest in extensive underground burrow system near water. *Range:* Inverness south to Olema, Marin County, and east to Lagunita. *Young:* 2 to 6 (usually 2 or 3) born in April. *Food:* Green vegetation (blackberry, ferns, nettle), bark.

Plate 1. Mule Deer and fawns in a redwood grove.

Plate 2. Raccoon (above).

A Long-tailed Weasel captures a Botta Pocket Gopher (below).

W.D. BERRY

Plate 3. Bobcat.

Plate 4.

Western Gray Squirrel

California Ground Squirrel   *Dusky-footed Wood Rat*

Plate 5.

Sonoma Chipmunk

California Pocket Mouse   Western Harvest Mouse
California Vole   Deer Mouse

Plate 6. *Gray Fox digging into a wood-rat house.*

Plate 7. Red Bat (above).

Heermann Kangaroo Rats pairing off to fight (below).

Plate 8. A Coyote closes in on a dodging Black-tailed Jack Rabbit.

CARNIVORES

The carnivores, or flesh-eating mammals, found in the bay region are cats, foxes, coyotes, skunks, badgers, weasels, and raccoons.

Mountain Lion, Cougar (*Felis concolor*)

The "mountain lions" reported in the bay region usually turn out to be bobcats or even house cats, but occasionally one really is seen. The presence of these big cats in this area is no cause for alarm, for there have been very few authenticated cases of one attacking a human. Shy and rarely observed, the lions may be found wherever there are deer. They are not necessarily dangerous to the deer population as a whole, for the deer they kill are frequently diseased or crippled.

Identification: Large; tawny coloration; long tail. Head and body 52 to 54 in. long; tail 30 to 36 in. long. Weighs 80 to 200 lbs. *Habitat:* Mountain, forest areas; dens in caves, crevices. *Range:* Dependent on the distribution and abundance of deer. *Young:* 1 to 4 (usually 2). *Food:* Chiefly deer, but also smaller mammals.

Bobcat, Wildcat (*Lynx rufus*)

Bobcats prefer to live in wooded ravines (pl. 3), but may choose any site that provides dense cover and an adequate food supply. Although Bobcats are relatively abundant in certain areas, they are seldom seen. They usually are more active at night, but occasionally come out in the daytime and sun themselves on exposed ledges and branches. However, their mottled coats blend so well with their surroundings that they may be very difficult to see.

Bobcats can hunt by day or night, for the vertical pupils of their eyes close to narrow slits in glaring sunlight or open wide to take full advantage of even dim starlight. The Bobcat's wide, soft paws conceal razor-sharp, retractile claws that can be brought into instant use. One of the identifying characteristics of

a cat's track is the absence of claw marks. When the cat walks, the claws are folded back against the toes.

As with most of the cat family, the responsibility of caring for the young is left to the female Bobcat. The young are born in the spring and summer and, like domestic kittens, they are helpless and their eyes are closed at birth. Kept in a well-hidden, secluded spot, the kittens remain with the mother until fall.

The male Bobcat is a solitary individual. If cornered, he can live up to his reputation as a fierce fighter, but ordinarily Bobcats go out of their way to avoid trouble. The Bobcats' chief enemies are men and dogs. The cats are hunted and trapped for their fur, and because of their reputation as killers of game birds and poultry. However, investigations have shown that most of their prey consists of rodents and rabbits.

Identification: Larger than house cat; tufted ears; short, bobbed tail. Head and body 25 to 30 in. long; tail 5 in. long. Weighs 15 to 30 lbs. *Habitat:* Dens usually in rocky crevices, hollow trees, or dense thickets in wooded and brushy areas. *Range:* Throughout the bay region. *Young:* One litter a year; 1 to 4 (average 3) in a litter. *Food:* Rodents, rabbits, other small mammals, and birds.

Gray Fox (*Urocyon cinereoargenteus*)

Gray Foxes, with their salt-and-pepper coats and inconspicuous ways, blend with the gray-greens of the chaparral. Well fitted for life in this tangled shrubbery, they can easily follow the network of trails and tunnels that honeycomb the underbrush. Sure-footed, they run along low branches or even climb into the trees. Their keen sense of smell and acute hearing help them locate the small rodents that make up much of their diet. A gaping hole in a wood-rat nest often means that a Gray Fox has been by (pl. 6).

Gray Foxes are an important part of the wildlife of this region. The number of harmful rodents they destroy each year is beneficial, particularly in agricultural areas. Their usefulness as rodent controllers far outweighs the occasional damage they do to game birds or poultry. Although Gray Foxes are fur bearers, their rusty and grizzled-gray pelts are not as valuable as those of the better-known Red Fox. The latter, a larger, golden-red animal, is not found in the bay region.

Both parents share in caring for their young, as do most members of the dog family. Fox pups become increasingly playful and adventurous as they grow, each trying to outrun, outclimb, and "outfox" the others. In many of their antics they resemble kittens more than puppies. At first the parents bring all the food to the den, but soon the pups are able to join on foraging trips, and each perfects his own skill as a hunter.

Identification: Grizzled-gray back, rusty-colored sides. Head and body 21 to 29 in. long; tail 11 to 16 in. long; height at shoulder 14 to 15 in. Weighs 7 to 13 lbs. *Habitat:* Prefers chaparral or chaparral-oak association. Den may be in crevices or under large rocks. *Range:* Throughout the bay region. *Young:* One litter a year; 2 to 5 in a litter. *Food:* Rodents, rabbits, fruits, and insects.

Coyote (*Canis latrans*)

Rolling grassy hills and open rangeland are the Coyote's favorite hunting grounds. Trotting with tail held low, he resembles a mistreated shepherd dog. His coat is usually unkempt and his hungry look is emphasized by his sharp features. His tongue hangs from his long muzzle; his pointed ears are alert for every sound. This appearance is deceiving, for he can cover many miles at a steady, apparently untiring trot, and in a burst of speed can overtake even a bounding jack rabbit (pl. 8). Often two or three Coyotes hunt together, seeming to find that teamwork produces better results. Quick to learn and adapt to changing conditions, the Coyote can hold his own even in settled areas. He is usually active between dusk and dawn, but is sometimes seen abroad during the day, especially in areas where he is unmolested. Coyotes are heard more often than seen. The setting sun or the first daylight may be greeted by a chorus of yap-

ping howls; often the entire choral effect comes from a single animal.

Unfortunately, some Coyotes add poultry and small livestock to their normal diet. As a result, Coyotes are shot, trapped, and poisoned. War against Coyotes continues even though studies have shown that nearly 80 per cent of their diet consists of jack rabbits, ground squirrels, gophers, mice, and similar small mammals. Much of the livestock that Coyotes are accused of killing is dead before they find it, and they are doing a service as scavengers by cleaning up the remains. Perhaps the best policy in dealing with Coyotes is to think before shooting; unless he is causing specific damage, a Coyote is probably doing a good job as a rodent exterminator.

Identification: Bushy tail, carried low when running. Head and body 32 to 37 in. long; tail 11 to 16 in. long; height at shoulder 23 to 26 in. Weighs 20 to 50 lbs. *Habitat:* Prefers open country or broken forest. May dig own den or use hollow log or tree. *Range:* Throughout the bay region. *Young:* One litter a year; 3 to 9 in a litter. *Food:* Primarily small mammals, carrion.

Striped Skunk (*Mephitis mephitis*)

The skunk's black-and-white pattern is a familiar warning to all. A sudden flare of his tail and stamping of his feet is the real danger signal, and any intruder foolish enough to venture closer will be sprayed with a nauseating oil. This offensive-smelling secretion is stored in two large glands opening near the base of the skunk's tail. With his powerful muscles, the skunk can squirt the oil accurately for a distance of ten feet.

Skunks are most frequently seen in late afternoon or evening as they start on their night's foraging. Since 50 per cent of their diet consists of insects, they are doing a service as they unconcernedly grub and dig for their favorite prey.

Identification: Black body with two white stripes. Head and body 13 to 18 in. long; tail 7 to 10 in. long. Weighs 6 to 10 lbs. *Habitat:* Riverbottom areas and semiopen country; avoids dense forests. Den under buildings, rock piles, or in old burrows. *Range:* Throughout the bay region. *Young:* One litter a year; 2 to 10 (average 4 to 5) in a litter. *Food:* Insects, fruits, rodents, and some birds.

Western Spotted Skunk (*Spilogale putorius*)

This small skunk is not so well known as the Striped Skunk, perhaps because of his more nocturnal habits. His defense is the same, but his warning is more spectacular. He not only raises his tail, but does a sort of war dance with his whole back end in the air (see sketch below). The Western Spotted Skunk has little value as a fur-bearer, but he is useful as a destroyer of insects and rodents.

Identification: Small; black body with broken white stripes. Head and body 9 to 13½ in. long; tail 4½ to 9 in. long. Weighs 1 to 2 lbs. *Habitat:* Prefers dry uplands; rocky, brushy country. Dens in hollow logs, old burrows, or under buildings and brush piles. *Range:* Throughout the bay region. *Young:* One litter born in the spring; 2 to 6 (average 4) in a litter. *Food:* Insects, fruits, small rodents, and birds.

Western Striped Skunk and Spotted Skunk

Badger (*Taxidea taxus*)

The hard, sun-baked soil of the rolling hills and open valleys is easy digging for a Badger. His squat form, short powerful legs, and long claws are well suited to a life of excavating and tunneling underground. In his search for burrowing rodents he leaves an unmistakable trail of potholes and piled earth. A cornered Badger has been known to dig himself to safety in a minute and a half. Even when caught above ground, he is a match for any dog. The Badger's diggings often make him unpopular with ranchers, who may overlook the fact that each excavation usually marks the end of a destructive rodent.

Identification: Flattened body; black-and-white face. Head and body 18 to 22 in. long; tail 4 to 6 in. long. Weighs 13 to 25 lbs. *Habitat:* Prefers open country; digs own burrow or den, 2 to 6 feet underground. *Range:* Throughout the bay region. *Young:* One litter a year; 1 to 4 in a litter. *Food:* Gophers, ground squirrels, other rodents, and reptiles.

Long-Tailed Weasel (*Mustela frenata*)

Like an undulating, golden-brown streak, a weasel bounds across a clearing and disappears into the vegetation. Soon his snakelike head reappears a short distance away; then he is on his way, investigating every gopher hole and mouse runway. The weasel is the only carnivore small enough to follow rats and mice into their burrows, and he hunts them either by day or night. He is found throughout the state, wherever there is water and ample food. Weasels are often destroyed as poultry killers, but studies have shown that this reputation is largely undeserved. More than 90 per cent of their diet consists of rodents (pl. 2).

Identification: Long slender body; black tip on tail. Head and body 8 to 10½ in. long; tail 3 to 6 in. long. Weighs 3 to 8 oz. (female smaller than male). *Habitat:* Wide variety of habitats; distribution dependent on abundance of rodents. Dens usually dug under stumps or rockslides. *Range:* Throughout the bay region. *Young:* One litter a year; 4 to 9 in a litter. *Food:* Small rodents, rabbits, and some birds.

Raccoon (*Procyon lotor*)

Raccoons leave their signatures, in the form of hand-like tracks, along muddy shores and stream banks. At night they patrol the waterways, wading in the shallows and "fishing." While fishing, the Raccoon rarely looks at what he is doing, relying mainly on his sense of touch (pl. 2). His sensitive paws explore underwater crevices, cray-fish holes, and tangles of water plants, and any frog or similar morsel his fingers touch is instantly seized. A Raccoon may "wash" this food before eating it, even though it just came out of the water. His washing habit may have nothing to do with cleaning the food, however, for the animals have been observed "washing" food in mud or even on dry ground.

Water also provides refuge for a cornered Raccoon. A pursuing dog may regret not giving up the chase at the water's edge, for the Raccoon is an efficient swimmer and often attempts to drown his opponent.

Identification: Black mask over eyes; banded tail. Head and body 18 to 28 in. long; tail 8 to 12 in. long. Weighs 12 to 35 lbs. *Habitat:* Found near lakes, rivers, creeks, and marshes; wooded areas. Usually dens in hollow trees or logs. *Range:* Throughout the bay region. *Young:* One litter a year; 3 to 7 in a litter. *Food:* Fish, frogs, fruit, insects, reptiles, and small mammals.

Ringtail (*Bassariscus astutus*)

This pretty animal is rarely seen, for it usually spends the day sleeping in a crevice or hollow tree. At night it emerges to hunt. Although it eats birds and some fruit, it is predominantly a mouser. For this reason early California miners frequently kept Ringtails as pets.

Identification: Long, ringed tail. Head and body 14 to 16 in. long; tail 15 in. long. *Habitat:* Wooded areas; prefers canyon walls with streams nearby. Dens in rocky crevices or hollow trees. *Range:* Throughout the bay region. Rare. *Young:* One litter a year; 1 to 5 in a litter. *Food:* Wood rats, mice, and other small rodents, fruit, and birds.

BATS

The bat's "hand" has developed into a wing, with the finger bones extended into long, thin supports for the wing membrane (see sketch above). Bats can see, but they usually fly in almost total darkness, and to avoid hitting obstacles they rely on a device similar to sonar. As it flies, the bat gives high-pitched "squeaks," which are sometimes keyed too high to be heard by our ears. These squeaks echo from objects in the bat's line of flight, and the returning sound warns him of obstacles. Bats are such skillful fliers that there is little chance of one ever getting caught in a person's hair. As the bats swoop around street lights on summer nights, they are capturing the flying insects attracted to the light. Bats are insectivorous, and do us a great service by destroying countless moths, mosquitoes, beetles, and other insects.

California Myotis (*Myotis californicus*)

The five other species of *Myotis* (see check list) found in the bay region are similar in appearance and habits to the California Myotis. Positive identification of specimens should be sought from a museum or university.

Identification: Tawny brown; face brownish (not blackish); ears and membranes dark. Head and body 2⁹⁄₁₀ to 3⅜ in. long. *Habitat:* Forages in wooded canyon bottoms, open forest, and over chaparral. Hides by day in rocky crevices, buildings, etc. *Range:* Throughout the bay region.

Big Brown Bat (*Eptesicus fuscus*)

Identification: Rich brown; larger than California Myotis; simple ear construction (see sketch below). Head and body 4 to 5 in. long. *Habitat:* Widespread; forages from forest lanes to open country. Hides by day in caves, rock crevices, buildings, etc.

Silver-haired Bat (*Lasionycteris noctivagans*)

Identification: Blackish brown, with silver-tipped hairs in middle of back. Head and body 4¼ in. long. *Habitat:* Forest borders; usually hangs in trees by day. *Range:* Sparingly distributed throughout bay region (summer and fall only).

Big Brown Bat   Myotis

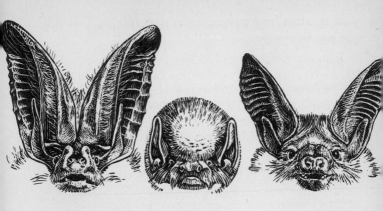

Long-eared Bat   Red Bat   Pallid Bat

Red Bat (*Lasiurus borealis*)

Identification: Reddish, with many white-tipped hairs; low, rounded ears (see above, and pl. 7). Head and body 3¾ to 4½ in. long. *Habitat:* Winter and spring: prefers deciduous growth along streams; hangs in trees, singly, by day. Summer and fall the males are found in wooded foothill areas; females at lower elevations. *Range:* Throughout the bay region.

Hoary Bat (*Lasiurus cinereus*)

Identification: Large; yellowish to mahogany brown with white-tipped hairs over most of the body. Head and body 5 to 5½ in. long. *Habitat:* Prefers open forest; hangs in trees, singly, by day. *Range:* Sparingly distributed throughout bay region; absent in summer.

Long-eared Bat (*Corynorhinus rafinesquei*)

Identification: Clove brown; lump on each side of muzzle; huge ears (more than 1 in.) joined across forehead (see sketch). Head and body 3½ to 4⅓ in. long. *Habitat:* Wooded areas. Roosts in dark places such as attics, and caves during day. *Range:* Throughout the bay region.

Pallid Bat (*Antrozous pallidus*)

Identification: Drab yellowish; large ears, *not* joined across forehead (see sketch opposite page). Head and body 4⅖ to 5 in. long. *Habitat:* Foothills; forages among trees or over open ground. Often roosts in attics, barns, etc. *Range:* Throughout the bay region.

Mexican Free-Tailed Bat (*Tadarida mexicana*)

Identification: Dull brown; tail projects beyond membrane connecting hind feet (see sketch). Head and body 3½ to 4 in. long; tail 1⅛ to 2½ in. long. *Habitat:* Widespread; forages in all habitats. Roosts in buildings, caves, and crevices, frequently in large colonies. *Range:* Throughout the bay region.

Mexican Free-tailed Bat

The insectivores, or insect-eating mammals, found in the bay region are shrews and moles. Although there are six species of shrews in the bay region (see check list), they are so much alike that positive identification of specimens should be sought from a museum or university.

Trowbridge Shrew (*Sorex trowbridgei*)

Although shrews are the smallest mammals in the bay region, they are active predators. A shrew darts nervously along tiny trails that are hidden under grass and fallen leaves, poking his flexible snout into every nook and cranny. He depends on his keen sense of smell to detect his prey, and will tackle insects of any size. Under his persistent attacks, even insects almost as large as the shrew are quickly killed and eaten. When the shrew finishes one meal, he is off hunting for the next one. Captive shrews have been known to die in a few hours when deprived of food.

Identification: Tapering snout; pinpoint eyes. Color uniformly brownish; bicolor tail. Head and body 2½ to 2⅖ in. long; tail 2 to 2½ in. long. *Habitat and range:* Coastal; canyon bottoms and chaparral slopes east to Berkeley. Often use mole or mouse burrows.

Young: One litter a year; usually 4 in a litter. *Food:* Insects, spiders, sow bugs, etc., Douglas Fir seeds.

Vagrant Shrew (*Sorex vagrans*)

Identification: Nearly black, or reddish brown above. Head and body 2⅓ to 2⅘ in. long; tail 1½ to 1⅘ in. long. *Habitat:* Humid coast belt; swampy or wet ground, under abundant cover, near sea level. *Range:* Salt marshes around south arm of San Francisco Bay.

Shrew-mole (*Neürotrichus gibbsi*)

The Shrew-mole, smallest of North American moles, spends much of his time above ground in a network of trails and tunnels beneath the leaves and tangled vegetation.

Identification: Black; forefeet longer than broad; tail relatively short, scaly, and haired. Head and body 3 to 3½ in. long; tail 1 to 1½ in. long. *Habitat:* Moist ground litter at edges of forest, around wet meadows, and along streams. *Range:* Restricted to humid coast belt, chiefly redwood forests. *Young:* Possibly several litters a year; 1 to 4 in a litter. *Food:* Earthworms, sow bugs, and insects.

Shrew-mole

Broad-footed Mole (*Scapanus latimanus*)

The mole is one of the strangest-looking mammals in the bay region. His eyes and ears are hidden by fur, and the palms of his front feet face outward and cannot be placed flat on the ground. However, the fur that hides his eyes and ears also keeps dirt out of them, and the mole has little need for good eyesight as he spends his life in darkness underground and finds his food by smell. His useless-looking front feet actually work like blades of a digging machine, and he can travel along his tunnels, or dig new ones, with amazing speed. Even the mole's fur is especially adapted for his life underground; because his fur will lie in either direction, he can run, unhindered, backward as well as forward in his narrow tunnels.

Long ridges on the surface of the ground are evidence of this animal's presence. These "runs" are his

feeding tunnels, which he pushes up just below the surface of the ground as he hunts for worms and insects. People often confuse the mole with the unrelated gopher. A gopher's tunnels (see p. 26) may be in constant use, but a mole run is often used only once. Thus a mole is hard to trap unless the trap is set in one of his main tunnels, which are deeper and more often used (see sketch). The dirt from these deeper tunnels is pushed to the surface in a "molehill"; unlike a gopher's mound, a molehill is never open.

Identification: Blackish brown with silvery sheen; eyes hidden; forefeet broader than long. Head and body 5 to 6 in. long; tail 1½ in. long. *Habitat:* Widespread; usually found in rich, moist ground. *Range:* Throughout the bay region. *Young:* One litter a year; 2 to 5 (average 4) in a litter. *Food:* Insects and worms.

OPOSSUM

Opossum (*Didelphis marsupialis*)

The Opossum, a marsupial (pouched mammal), is not native to California, but was introduced from the eastern United States around 1900. Since then, opossums have spread over most of the state, and have become well established. They can eat almost anything, and can hunt food equally well on the ground or in trees.

Opossums often wander into garages, under houses, or in front of moving automobiles. When discovered, they usually feign ferocity with gaping jaws and threatening hisses, but often they merely topple over on their sides. With eyes half closed, tongues lolling out, and jaws drooling, they seem to be dead. If undisturbed, most Opossums soon revive and go about their business. "Playing 'possum" may be a method of defense, or possibly a state of fainting. Probably an Opossum's chief protection is its habit of freezing if danger is near, then retreating so slowly and silently that it remains unnoticed.

Like the distantly related kangaroo, the female Opossum carries her young in a pouch. Newborn Opossums are so tiny that more than a dozen would fit in a teaspoon. After a month they are about the size of mice, and by the time they are three months old they are too large to fit comfortably in the pouch. Then the mother carries them clinging to her fur—not hanging from her tail, as is often supposed.

Identification: Prehensile, naked tail; white face, gray body. Head and body 15 to 20 in. long; tail 9 to 13 in. long. Weighs 4 to 12 lbs. *Habitat:* Prefers cultivated lowlands, foothill areas near streams. Dens in hollow logs, trees, under buildings, or in old burrows. *Range:* Throughout the bay region. *Young:* Two litters a year; 4 to 13 (average 7) in a litter. *Food:* Anything edible: fruits, nuts, eggs, carrion, etc.

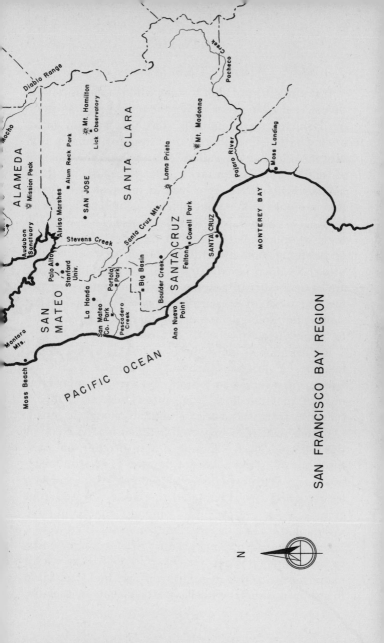

ACTIVITIES

WHERE TO SEE MAMMALS

It is a real test of skill to spot wild mammals out-of-doors. Your chances of seeing them are better at dawn or dusk, for many animals start to feed and move around just before sunrise and sunset. (Animals that are active by day are called "diurnal," and those active at night are "nocturnal.") Because most of these animals will see or hear you before you see them, they are able to keep out of your sight. The best way to observe mammals is to hide yourself and wait for them to appear. Sit quietly at the edge of a clearing or beside a trail; after about fifteen or twenty minutes the animal activity that was interrupted by your appearance should resume. Many mammals are not disturbed even if you are reading, writing, or moving slowly, but sudden motions or sharp sounds are sure to alarm them.

Seeing animals at night is easier than one might imagine. A bright (focusing) flashlight is all the equipment needed to "shine" the eyes of animals at night. Often the light from automobile headlights is reflected from the eyes of animals along the road. Different mammals may be identified by the color of this reflected "flash." A green or amber reflection often turns out to be the color (of the eyes) of a wandering house cat. With experience at "shining" you can learn to recognize the characteristic flashes of different animals. Pick an area for "shining" that you have visited in the daytime, and that you know, from tracks, scats (animals droppings), cuttings, burrows, or nests, to be occupied. When you have located areas where mammals are active at night, you may find it possible to set up a camera with flash attachments so that the mammals take their own pictures (see suggested references, p. 70).

There are many areas where wild mammals can be found within city limits. Skunks, raccoons, and opossums often visit garbage cans in search of scraps. Vacant lots, parks, brushy canyons, and similar places afford shelter for many mammals.

In another book of this series, *Introduction to the Natural History of the San Francisco Bay Region,* you will find a list of field trips for seeing wildlife.

If you are interested in any particular mammal, the range and habitat descriptions in this book will tell you the type of country where you might find it. In addition, the following are places where wild mammals are frequently seen:

East Bay—Strawberry Canyon, University of California, East Bay Regional Parks, and Mount Diablo State Park.

Marin County—Muir Woods, Mount Tamalpais, and Samuel Taylor State Park.

San Francisco—Golden Gate Park and Seal Rocks.

Peninsula Area—Big Basin State Park, La Honda, Portola State Park, and Moss Landing.

San Jose—Alum Rock Park and Mount Hamilton.

MAMMAL TRACKS

Frequently a mammal's story may be recorded in the tracks it leaves. There are several good books dealing with this subject (see p. 70). Mammal tracks are often found near burrows, in the dust along trails, or under sheltering boulders or logs. Mammal tracks along a stream or in the mud around a puddle can be permanently reproduced in plaster.

The following inexpensive materials are needed for track casting: (1) A low wall of cardboard (cross-

Casting a mammal track in plaster.

section of milk carton) or tin, pressed into the mud around the track to keep the plaster from spreading too far (see sketch A). (2) Container to mix the plaster and water (old coffee can). (3) Water—the amount depends on the size of the cast: one-half cup is enough for a cup of plaster. (4) Plaster of Paris (approximately 1 cup for a dog- or deer-size track), *added to the water* until the mixture is about as thick as a milkshake (see sketch B). A few taps on the container before pouring will release air bubbles that might spoil the cast. Pour the mixture, smooth the top of the cast, and when it is firm scratch the date, place, and name of the mammal on each cast. In a few minutes the plaster will be hard enough for the cast to be lifted from the original track (see sketch C). When the plaster has dried, any adhering mud can be scrubbed off with a toothbrush and water. This cast is a negative cast. To make a positive track, repeat the above procedure, using the negative cast as a model (see sketch p. 69). Be *sure* to brush liquid soap or thin oil on the old cast so the new plaster will lift off without sticking.

Taking Notes

There are still many facts about the lives of wild mammals that have not been observed and recorded. A carefully kept notebook of accurate field observations may add to our knowledge of American wildlife.

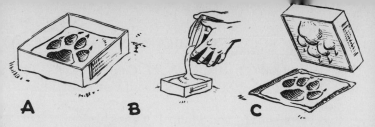

Making a negative cast from a positive cast.

The notes need not be elaborate; the best scientific observations are brief and to the point. They tell exactly what was seen and the conditions (date, time, place, weather) under which it was seen. Use a separate page for each species. The outline below is standard for taking field notes.

CAPTIVE MAMMALS

Most wild mammals do not make good pets. Wild adult mammals are rarely tameable. Even small mammals such as the rodents may be dangerous to handle, not only because of their sharp teeth but because they often harbor disease-carrying ticks or fleas. Occasionally, very young mammals are found that can be successfully raised. Diluted canned milk, fed every few hours with an eyedropper or a baby bottle, works well for most baby mammals; as they grow older, their natural diets should be followed as closely as possible. They need plenty of exercise space and cages that can be scrubbed regularly. Remember that in captivity a wild animal loses most of its natural alertness, and if returned to the wild is often unable to find food and shelter, or becomes easy prey for some predator.

Bob Jones '59	Black-tailed Deer 2
Feb 19	Wildcat Creek, Contra Costa Co., Calif.
2:30 PM	A buck was seen bounding into heavy chaparral. He was in his winter coat but had shed one antler.
June 12	Muir Woods, Marin Co., Calif. A doe
7:15 AM	and two young fawns were seen near road; doe was browsing on

SUGGESTED REFERENCES

Ingles, Lloyd G. *Mammals of California and its Coastal Waters.* Stanford: Stanford University Press, 1954.

Burt, William H., and Philip P. Grossenheider. *Field Guide to the Mammals.* New York: Houghton Mifflin, 1952.

Cahalane, Victor H. *Mammals of North America.* New York: Macmillan, 1947.

Murie, Olaus J. *A Field Guide to Animal Tracks.* New York: Houghton Mifflin, 1954.

Moore, Clifford B. *Book of Wild Pets.* Boston: Charles P. Branford Company, 1954.

Hillcourt, William. *Field Book of Nature Activities.* New York: G. P. Putnam's Sons, 1950.

CHECK LIST OF BAY REGION MAMMALS

The following list includes all species of mammals regularly found in the ten counties of the San Francisco Bay region. After the name of each mammal described in the text is the page number of the description. For the mammals not described in this book, a brief summary of their range is given.

ORDER MARSUPIALIA
Opossum (*Didelphis marsupialis*), p. 62.

ORDER INSECTIVORA
Broad-footed Mole (*Scapanus latimanus*), p. 60.

Shrew-mole (*Neürotrichus gibbsi*), p. 59.

Trowbridge Shrew (*Sorex trowbridgei*), p. 58.

Vagrant Shrew (*S. vagrans*), p. 59.

Pacific Shrew (*S. pacificus*). Moist ground under dense vegetation; coastal; not found south of Marin Co.

Adorned Shrew (*S. ornatus*). Streams and damp places throughout bay region.

Suisun Shrew (*S. sinuosus*). Known only from Grizzly Island, Suisun Bay.

Pacific Water Shrew (*S. bendirei*). Swampy places; coastal area south to extreme northern Sonoma Co.

ORDER CHIROPTERA

Little Brown Myotis (*Myotis lucifugus*). Ranges south to Sonoma and Napa counties; forested areas. (See p. 55.)

Yuma Myotis (*M. yumanensis*). Throughout bay region.

Long-eared Myotis (*M. evotis*). Throughout bay region.

Fringed Myotis (*M. thysanodes*). Throughout bay region.

Long-legged Myotis (*M. volans*). Throughout bay region.

California Myotis (*M. californicus*), p. 54.

Western Pipistrelle *Pipistrellus hesperus*). Found in arid areas south of the bay; in Napa Co. north of bay.

Big Brown Bat (*Eptesicus fuscus*), p. 55.

Silver-haired Bat (*Lasionycteris noctivagans*), p. 55.

Hoary Bat (*Lasiurus cinereus*), p. 56.

Red Bat (*L. borealis*), p. 56, pl. 7.

Long-eared Bat (*Corynorhinus rafinesquei*), p. 56.

Pallid Bat (*Antrozous pallidus*), p. 57.

Mexican Free-tailed Bat (*Tadarida mexicana*), p. 57.

ORDER CARNIVORA

Black Bear (*Ursus americanus*). Sonoma Co.; rare.

Raccoon (*Procyon lotor*), p. 52, pl. 2.

Ringtail (*Bassariscus astutus*), p. 53.

Ermine (*Mustela erminea*). Extreme northern Sonoma Co.

Long-tailed Weasel (*M. frenata*), p. 51, pl. 2.

Mink (*M. vison*). Marshes, stream sides, and tidal sloughs as far south as Marin Co.

River Otter (*Lutra canadensis*). Streams and fresh-water marshes as far south as Drake's Bay, Marin Co.

Western Spotted Skunk (*Spilogale putorius*), p. 49.

Striped Skunk (*Mephitis mephitis*), p. 48.

Badger (*Taxidea taxus*), p. 50.

Gray Fox (*Urocyon cinereoargenteus*), p. 44, pl. 6.

Coyote (*Canis latrans*), p. 46, pl. 8.

Mountain Lion or Cougar (*Felis concolor*), p. 41.

Bobcat or Wildcat (*Lynx rufus*), p. 42, pl. 3.

SUBORDER PINNIPEDIA

California Sea Lion (*Zalophus californianus*). Seacoast.

Northern Sea Lion or Steller Sea Lion (*Eumetopias jubata*). Seacoast; often seen on Seal Rocks, San Francisco.

Harbor Seal (*Phoca vitulina*). Seacoast; harbors, bays, islands.

ORDER RODENTIA

California Ground Squirrel (*Citellus beecheyi*), p. 31, pl. 4.

Townsend Chipmunk (*Eutamias townsendi*). Open forest, Sonoma Co.

Sonoma Chipmunk (*E. sonomae*), p. 30, pl. 5.

Merriam Chipmunk (*E. merriami*). Chaparral slopes south of San Francisco Bay (similar to *E. sonomae*).

Douglas Squirrel *or* Chickaree (*Tamiasciurus douglasi*). Open forest, Sonoma Co.

Western Gray Squirrel (*Sciurus griseus*), p. 28, pl. 4.

Eastern Gray Squirrel (*S. carolinensis*), p. 29.

Fox Squirrel (*S. niger*), p. 29.

Botta Pocket Gopher (*Thomomys bottae*), p. 26, pl. 2.

San Joaquin Pocket Mouse (*Perognathus inornatus*), p. 25.

California Pocket Mouse (*P. californicus*), p. 25, pl. 5.

Heermann Kangaroo Rat (*Dipodomys heermanni*), p. 24, pl. 7.

Narrow-faced Kangaroo Rat (*D. venustus*). Chaparral-covered areas south from southern San Mateo Co.; also Mt. Hamilton.

Western Harvest Mouse (*Reithrodontomys megalotis*), p. 17, pl. 5.

Salt-marsh Harvest Mouse (*R. raviventris*), p. 17.

California Mouse (*Peromyscus californicus*), p. 19.

Deer Mouse (*P. maniculatus*), p. 18, pl. 5.

Brush Mouse (*P. boylei*). Woodland and tall chaparral south as far as the Vaca Mountains, Napa Co.

Piñon Mouse (*P. truei*), p. 19.

Desert Wood Rat (*Neotoma lepida*), p. 21.

Dusky-footed Wood Rat *or* Pack Rat (*N. fuscipes*), p. 20, pl. 4.

Red Tree Mouse (*Phenacomys longicaudus*). Found in Douglas Fir and Grand Fir forests, from the Russian River area north.

Western Red-backed Mouse (*Clethrionomys occidentalis*). Coastal; coniferous forest south to Sonoma Co.

California Vole *or* California Meadow Mouse (*Microtus californicus*), p. 22, pl. 5.

Muskrat (*Ondatra zibethica*). Introduced; now found in many rivers and fresh-water marshes.

Norway Rat (*Rattus norvegicus*), p. 14.

Black Rat *or* Roof Rat (*R. rattus*), p. 15.

House Mouse (*Mus musculus*), p. 16.

Aplodontia *or* Mountain Beaver (*Aplodontia rufa*), p. 32.

Pacific Jumping Mouse (*Zapus trinotatus*). Grassy, marshy areas, southern and western Marin Co.

ORDER LAGOMORPHA

Black-tailed Jack Rabbit (*Lepus californicus*), p. 12, pl. 8.

Desert Cottontail (*Sylvilagus auduboni*), p. 10.

Brush Rabbit (*S. bachmani*), p. 11.

ORDER ARTIODACTYLA

Mule Deer *or* Black-tailed Deer (*Odocoileus hemionus*), p. 8, pl. 1.

ORDER CETACEA

Pacific Harbor Porpoise (*Phocaena vomerina*). Ocean and bay.